Fiction
at this level

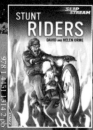

STUNT **RIDERS**
DAVID AND HELEN ORME
978 1 4451 1314 2 pb

UNARMED AND **DANGEROUS**
DAVID AND HELEN ORME
978 1 4451 1316 6 pb

WALK INTO **DANGER**
DAVID AND HELEN ORME
978 1 4451 1318 0 pb

ROBBED!
ANNE CASSIDY
978 1 4451 1815 4 pb

WOLFHOLD
STEVE BARLOW AND STEVE SKIDMORE
978 1 4451 1814 7 pb

WHITE WATER **WIPE OUT!**
ROGER HURN
978 1 4451 1816 1 pb

Graphic fiction
at this level

ALIEN **CAGE**
JONNY ZUCKER AND MKU
978 1 4451 1322 7 pb

FUTURE **TENSE**
JONNY ZUCKER AND LEO CARTER
978 1 4451 1320 3 pb

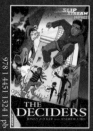

THE **DECIDERS**
JONNY ZUCKER AND ANDREW LYDE
978 1 4451 1324 1 pb

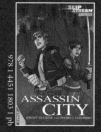

ASSASSIN **CITY**
JONNY ZUCKER AND PEDRO J. COLOMBO
978 1 4451 1803 1 pb

SWORD OF **LEGEND**
JONNY ZUCKER AND LENARO WHITE
978 1 4451 1802 4 pb

SWITCH **FACE**
JONNY ZUCKER AND KEV HOPGOOD
978 1 4451 1804 8 pb

Non-fiction
at this level

SUPER **ANIMALS**
ANNE ROONEY
978 1 4451 1358 6 pb

WORLD'S **FASTEST**
ANNE ROONEY
978 1 4451 1360 9 pb

GREATEST ROCK **BANDS**
ANNE ROONEY
978 1 4451 1310 4 hb
978 1 4451 1359 3 pb

SPACE
ANNE ROONEY
978 1 4451 1956 4 hb

DARING **ESCAPES**
ANNE ROONEY
978 1 4451 1957 1 hb

HOW TO SPEND **A BILLION**
ANNE ROONEY
978 1 4451 1955 7 hb

SLIP STREAM

DARING ESCAPES »»

ANNE ROONEY

EDGE FRANKLIN WATTS

LONDON·SYDNEY

Disclaimer — The activities depicted in this book were carried out in extreme circumstances. Don't copy them. The Author and Publishers regret that they can accept no liability for any loss or injury sustained.

First published in 2013 by
Franklin Watts
338 Euston Road
London NW1 3BH

Franklin Watts Australia
Level 17/207 Kent Street
Sydney NSW 2000

© Franklin Watts 2013

(ebook) ISBN: 978 1 4451 2909 9
(hb) ISBN: 978 1 4451 1957 1
(library ebook) ISBN: 978 1 4451 2590 9

Dewey classification number: 428.6

A CIP catalogue record for this book is available from the British Library.

Series Editors: Adrian Cole and Jackie Hamley
Series Advisors: Diana Bentley and Dee Reid
Series Designer: Peter Scoulding
Picture Researcher: Diana Morris

Printed in China

Franklin Watts is a division of Hachette Children's Books, an Hachette UK company.
www.hachette.co.uk

Acknowledgements:
Alamy Celebrity/Alamy: 11.
Greg Amptman/Shutterstock: 1, 6br.
AP/PAI: 19.
AP/Topham: 23.
Curioso/Shutterstock: 22.
Gustavo Fernandes/Dreamstime: 6bl.
Andreas Fischer/Dreamstime: 17.
Government of Chile/Corbis: front cover.
Keystone USA-ZUMA/Rex Features: 4.
Cezaro de Luca/epa/Corbis: 5.
Ali Mufti/Shutterstock: 16.
Pictorial Press/Alamy: 12, 13, 15.
Picturpoint/Topfoto: 21.
Paul Topp/Dreamstime: 7.
urosr/Shutterstock: 18.
Beth Wald/Aurora Photos/Alamy: 8, 9, 10.
Christian Wilkinson/Shutterstock: 14.

Every attempt has been made to clear copyright. Should there be any inadvertent omission, please apply to the publisher for rectification.

CONTENTS

ARE YOU A SURVIVOR?

Some people survive terrible things. Thirty-three Chilean miners were trapped in their mine when it fell in. For 17 days, no one knew they were alive.

Then it took 52 days to rescue them.

SHARK ALERT

Bethany Hamilton likes to surf. When she was 13, a shark bit off her arm. She paddled to shore using the other arm. She still surfs! Would you?

ROCK HARD

Aron Ralston was climbing when his arm got stuck under a rock. For six days he hoped for rescue. No one came. He scratched his name in the rock.

Then Aron had an idea. He bent his arm to break the bone. Then he cut his arm off with his knife. It took an hour. At last, he walked free and found help.

OVER THE ICE

Ernest Shackleton led explorers to the South Pole in 1914. Their ship was crushed in the ice. They were stranded.

They camped on floating ice for four months.

Then the ice broke up. They got into the lifeboats. After five days they reached an island. But no one lived there. So Shackleton and five other men went for help.

They rowed 1,500 km to another island. Then they walked for 36 hours. At last, they found help!

LOST!

Robbers stole Ricky Megee's car. They dumped him in the Australian outback. He was totally lost. He ate lizards, insects and dried frogs. He chewed raw leeches.

Ricky had to pull out a rotten tooth using a car key. After 71 days, men in a car rescued him. He was so thin that he weighed only half his usual weight.

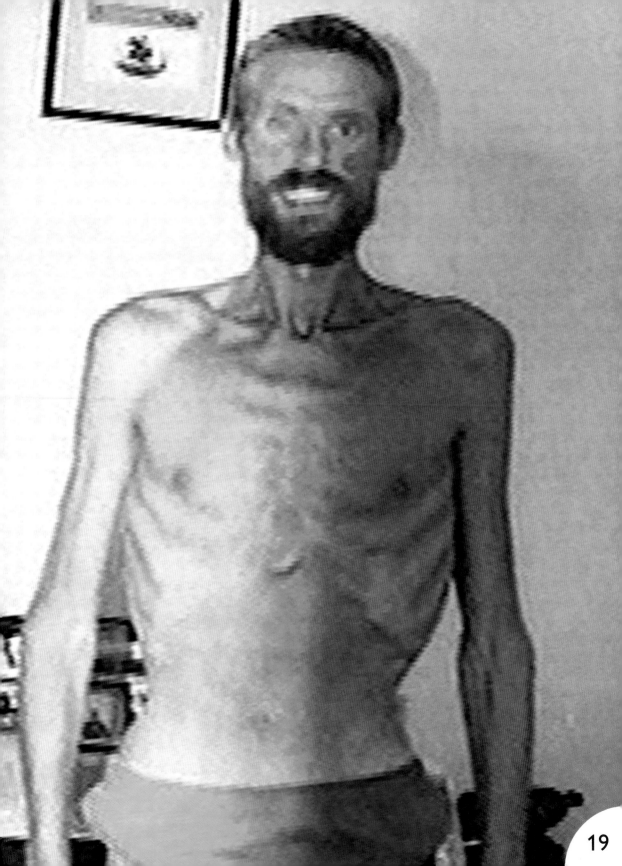

PLANE CRASH

In 1972, a plane crashed into freezing mountains in Chile. Sixteen people died. Only 29 survived.

The survivors heard a
message on their radio.
It said that the search for
them had stopped.

The survivors soon ran out food. They had to eat their dead friends. At last, two of them crossed the mountains and got help.

Helicopters were sent for the others.

Could you survive a daring escape?

INDEX

FOR TEACHERS

About

Slipstream is a series of expertly levelled books designed for pupils who are struggling with reading. Its unique three-strand approach through fiction, graphic fiction and non-fiction gives pupils a rich reading experience that will accelerate their progress and close the reading gap.

At the heart of every Slipstream non-fiction book is exciting information. Easily accessible words and phrases ensure that pupils both decode and comprehend, and the topics really engage older struggling readers.

Whether you're using Slipstream Level 1 for Guided Reading or as an independent read, here are some suggestions:

1. Make each reading session successful. Talk about the text before the pupil starts reading. Introduce any unfamiliar vocabulary.

2. Encourage the pupil to talk about the book using a range of open questions. For example, what is the most daring escape they can think of?

3. Discuss the differences between reading non-fiction, fiction and graphic fiction. What do they prefer?

For guidance, SLIPSTREAM Level 1 – Daring Escapes has been approximately measured to:

National Curriculum Level: 2c
Reading Age: 7.0–7.6
Book Band: Turquoise

ATOS: 2.0*
Guided Reading Level: H
Lexile® Measure (confirmed): 370L

Slipstream Level photocopiable **WORKBOOK 2** ISBN: 978 1 4451 1798 0 available – download free sample worksheets from: www.franklinwatts.co.uk

*Please check actual Accelerated Reader™ book level and quiz availability at www.arbookfind.co.uk